Communities of Practice

A GUIDE FOR YOUR JOURNEY TO KNOWLEDGE MANAGEMENT BEST PRACTICES

Farida Hasanali

Cindy Hubert

Kimberly Lopez

Bob Newhouse

Carla O'Dell

Wesley Vestal

AMERICAN PRODUCTIVITY
& QUALITY CENTER

American Productivity & Quality Center
123 North Post Oak Lane, Third Floor
Houston, Texas 77024

Edited by Craig Henderson and Paige Leavitt
Designed by Connie Choate

Manufactured in the United States of America

ISBN 1-928593-48-8

American Productivity & Quality Center
Web site address: www.apqc.org

Contents

Acknowledgments

The American Productivity & Quality Center (APQC) would like to thank all of the organizations we have worked with to uncover trends, working models, and best practices in fostering communities of practice. Without the organizations that sponsor our research—and especially those that are willing to impart their knowledge, experiences, and insights—we would not be able to share this valuable information with the public.

We are especially grateful to the sponsors and partners of our consortium benchmarking effort, *Building and Sustaining Communities of Practice: Continuing Success in Knowledge Management* (2000). A significant amount of information in this book was gained from partner organizations that allowed our study team to examine and learn from their communities of practice initiatives.

Some of the organizations from which we have learned a great deal include the following:
- AT&T
- Accenture
- Best Buy Company
- BP Amoco
- British Telecom
- Buckman Laboratories
- Cap Gemini Ernst & Young
- Chevron
- Compaq
- DaimlerChrysler Corporation

- Dow Corning Corporation
- Ford Motor Company
- General Electric
- IBM/Lotus
- Johnson Controls
- MITRE Corporation
- Motorola
- Schlumberger
- Siemens AG
- The World Bank Group
- Xerox Corporation

Preface

S everal years ago the American Productivity & Quality Center began to notice how important communities of practice were in creating, gathering, and sharing knowledge as part of formal knowledge management (KM) efforts. Deciding to examine communities in detail to better understand their nature, their role, and how to create and successfully sustain them, APQC conducted what, to our knowledge, is the largest single study of communities of practice to date, *Building and Sustaining Communities of Practice* (2000). In addition to our extensive research, APQC also has worked side by side with many organizations, public and private, to design and implement communities.

Our research and experiences provide compelling evidence that communities are assuming a new role in knowledge work and KM systems. Community activities also are becoming embedded in the daily work of knowledge workers.

The purpose of this book is to provide an overview of and introduction to communities of practice. It can be used to start the reader on a learning path, or it can be offered to colleagues and executives who need an education on the topic but may not have time to explore it in great detail. Throughout this book, APQC will provide information about resources that will take the reader and practitioner deeper into the subject of how to create communities that provide value to their members and to the organization.

APQC'S PASSPORT TO SUCCESS

Since 1977 the mission of APQC has been to create and disseminate knowledge to help organizations perform more effectively. We've done that in numerous ways over the years, from developing improvement and measurement approaches to offering benchmarking studies, conferences, training courses, research services, and a variety of publications.

Our members and other customers have expressed a need for easy-to-use, inexpensive resource guides to understand and implement programs and processes in a variety of functional areas. As a result, we've drawn on our experience and knowledge to produce APQC's Passport to Success book series.

The books that make up this series are intended to guide you on what can be a journey through somewhat foreign territory. Each provides readers with the mechanisms to gauge their current status, understand the components (or landmarks) of a successful initiative in a specific topic area, and determine how to proceed within their own organization.

Passport to Success series titles supplement other educational products and services APQC offers so that we may be your one-stop source for process improvement tools. Please visit our Web site at www.apqc.org or call 800-776-9676 (713-681-4020 outside the United States) to learn more.

Why Cultivate Communities of Practice?

People have always created communities, inside and outside of organizations. What is emerging in the new workplace, and in knowledge management (KM) initiatives, is the prominence and formality of communities of practice as boundary-spanning units in organizations, responsible for finding and sharing best practices, stewarding knowledge, and helping community members work better. This new role for communities is emerging because they consciously nurture and harness knowledge in service of the organization.

Why are communities becoming so important? The defining feature of communities is that they cross boundaries created by workflow, functions, geography, and time. In the modern, knowledge-based, global organization, communities create a channel for knowledge to flow across the boundaries. Cap Gemini Ernst & Young communities are organized by region, service lines, and industry; DaimlerChrysler tech clubs share design know-how across platform teams; Ford's best-practice replication communities facilitate adoption of proven practices across plants; the World Bank's thematic groups share knowledge in pursuit of the eradication of poverty around the world; and Xerox service technicians share repair tips across their global Eureka network.

These few examples reveal another feature of communities: they provide the means to move local know-how to collective information and promote standardization of practices across operations and regions.

A less tangible, but equally as important feature of communities is that they strengthen the social fabric of the organization, a fabric that may have been worn thin by geography and size. People share a common interest, legitimized by business intent, and form relationships that provide social support, excitement, and personal validation. Members collaborate, use one another as sounding boards, teach each other, and strike out together to explore new subject matter.

It has become conventional wisdom that organizations must capitalize on knowledge to be fast, innovative, and successful. Traditional organizational forms, which stressed hierarchy and chains of command, have given way to more decentralized forms of management.

Organizations have embraced communities of practice because they enable knowledge-sharing relationships, accelerate learning, and enhance successful implementation. Organizations that want to seize opportunities associated with knowledge management depend on communities of practice to propel such critical initiatives.

Definition of Communities

Networks of people—small and large—who come together to share ideas with and learn from one another in physical and virtual space. These communities of practice, of interest, and of learning are held together by a common purpose or mission. They are sustained by a desire to share experiences, insights, and best practices.

WHAT ARE COMMUNITIES OF PRACTICE?

Quite simply, a community of practice is a group of people that shares an expertise and is bound by a common mission or purpose. Members identify with the group's expertise and seek to enhance their own. Unlike teams or workgroups, they are not bound by a fixed project, agenda, or set of deliverables. They produce information, insights, and best practices—simply put, knowledge.

Communities of practice may exist within organizations or stretch across organizational boundaries. Stock traders, direct marketers, heart surgeons, oil drillers, copier technicians, personal-injury lawyers, Freudian psychologists, financial journalists, real estate salespeople, and Java programmers have counted themselves as members of such communities.

Communities also tend to arise within organizations around certain professional needs and experiences, like finance, marketing, information technology, sales, and customer care. We find them also developing from new organizational opportunities or initiatives—be it e-business, customer intimacy, or knowledge management.

Communities of practice go by many names. In the World Bank, they are called thematic groups. At Ford, they are called best-practice teams. DaimlerChrysler refers to them as Tech Clubs. And in many consulting firms they are called knowledge networks. Communities of practice are being recognized as a new organizational form that complements existing structures. They do not necessarily replace other organizational arrangements; they merely promise to enhance the capabilities of an organization by addressing the unmet needs of the individuals within it.

Within this definition, we can assess how influential communities have become. They are the shadow networks within and beyond organizations. They may or may not be acknowledged on organizational charts and in explicit hierarchies, but they are nevertheless potentially powerful.

Communities of practice are important for additional reasons. Members of communities offer insights, answers, and solutions.

People turn to them to figure out how to address challenging business problems. And once a community has been established, individuals can seek assistance from other members—wherever they are. Sometimes that means walking down the hall. Sometimes it means posting a request on a special Web site devoted to the community.

Communities of practice consist of people who help us develop our crafts and excel as practitioners. And it's important to point out that learning is not the same thing as training. We can't easily learn the most important things, such as cutting-edge practices and tricks of the trade, from a training course. We tend to learn most effectively as part of a community.

Some organizations are beginning to realize that they can make the most of this phenomenon by cultivating existing networks. With communities becoming such a key component in organizations' knowledge management initiatives, a number of organizations have responded with financial resources.

However, there's more to supporting communities than just money. It requires leadership, sponsorship, and the active involvement of members. It also requires a supportive infrastructure with tools, technology, and resources. As organizations invest in these communities, they assume more formal sponsorship arrangements and establish more explicit roles and responsibilities.

Although some organizations have chosen to keep communities informal, APQC's work and research in knowledge management indicate that best-practice organizations are guiding communities to become a formalized part of their approach toward innovation and technical excellence.

Drawing on the insights acquired through APQC's years of knowledge management experience and its recent multiclient benchmarking study, *Building and Sustaining Communities of Practice*, this book will offer some valuable perspectives, frameworks, and best practices to help you cultivate effective communities of practice in your organization. We cite examples throughout the book based on the real-world experiences of numerous organizations that partici-

> The idea that an organization is a constellation of 'Communities of Practice' is a genuine breakthrough. ... It is an idea that has profound implications for what it takes to run a successful organization in our frenetic, chaotic times."
>
> —Tom Peters, author, *In Search of Excellence*

pated in our research: AT&T; Accenture; BP Amoco; British Telecom; Cap Gemini Ernst & Young; DaimlerChrysler; Ford Motor; IBM/Lotus; Schlumberger; Siemens; The World Bank Group; and Xerox. As the experiences of these organizations powerfully demonstrate, extraordinary returns can be generated by forward-looking investments in communities of practice.

The following findings, statements, and observations stem from our research; each will be explored in more detail in subsequent chapters.

1. Best-practice organizations strategically select communities of practice to support, based on importance to the business and the business opportunity.

2. During our research, we have used a framework for types of communities developed by Richard McDermott, which categorizes communities by their primary business intent:

   a) to provide a forum for community members to help each other solve everyday work problems;

   b) to develop and disseminate best practices, guidelines, and procedures for their members to use;

   c) to organize, manage, and steward a body of knowledge from which community members can draw; and

   d) to innovate and create breakthrough ideas, knowledge, and practices.

Most communities serve more than one of these purposes, but one intent usually dominates the design choices made to support a community. These differences have significant implications for the design and preparation of communities. For example, a technical community whose intent is to steward and grow the body of knowledge in their discipline will have different processes than a community with the intent to simply provide help to community members.

3. For sustaining a community, senior management is not the most important critical success factor. Management is instrumental in selecting communities, ensuring their link to business opportunities, and providing resources. Once the communities are selected, however, the most critical success factor (there are many) is the skill of the community leader.

4. As evidence of the rising importance of communities in the knowledge work of organizations, 74 percent of best-practice organizations report that operating units rely on communities to provide knowledge resources, and 66 percent of them said that communities set standards that operating units need to follow.

5. Communities use a rich variety of media to communicate and work. The most frequently used tool for communication is e-mail. Many also use specialized KM community tools. E-mail appears to augment KM tools and integrate community work into day-to-day work. However, when rating the effectiveness of media, partners still rate face-to-face interaction as most effective, followed closely by a dedicated KM tool. This mixture of applications and media increases the richness of interaction within a community, rather than replacing other media.

6. Organizations provide significant support resources to communities in the form of content managers and systems, community coordinators, and information technology applications. Models for support and funding vary, as does the amount and nature of support resources required by community type. All depend on some central resources, especially at the beginning for consulting, training, and content management. Business units typically

underwrite the costs for their participants' time and for leader and SME participation. Once communities are well established, the business units usually underwrite the central costs through direct billing or overhead allocation. Communities are included in the budgeting and planning process as a regular feature.

7. In order to become institutionalized, communities need to have a link to the formal organization. Although communities of practice tend to be boundary-spanning entities, their support structures tend to be tightly linked to and integrated with the formal organizational structure. This provides legitimacy and the link to management support, funding, and shared resources.

8. Membership requirements vary greatly across organizations, from voluntary to strongly encouraged to mandatory, especially in the case of many consulting firms.

9. Communities tend to be more member-driven and democratic than the formal organization structure. At Schlumberger, communities elect their leaders through formal balloting processes. At Xerox, one community rebelled against too much management oversight and demanded that it be allowed to self-manage and only be accountable for results.

10. There are two major categories of community measurement: assessing health and measuring impact. Appropriate measures are a direct reflection of the type of community.

Where Are You Now?

The following quiz is designed to help you determine the current state of knowledge management as it relates to fostering communities of practice in your organization. Answer these questions, and then score your organization based on the scale on page 10 to determine your point of origination.

1. Is your organization's environment conducive to establishing networks of people with common interests, problems, tasks, etc.?

   Yes ☐   No ☐

2. Have any communities of practice been identified within your organization?

   Yes ☐   No ☐

3. Is there a general consensus within your organization that communities of practice are important?

   Yes ☐   No ☐

4. Is there any formal sponsorship and/or financial backing for communities of practice among senior executives in your organization?

   Yes ☐   No ☐

5. Is there widespread recognition of the value of communities within your organization?

   Yes ☐   No ☐

6. Have any formal roles or responsibilities emerged and/or been assigned within your organization's communities?

   Yes ☐   No ☐

7. Are there any regular meetings, conferences, or forums where members of communities can meet and share knowledge?

    Yes ☐ No ☐

8. Are there any efforts under way to assess or measure the value of communities of practice within your organization?

    Yes ☐ No ☐

9. Are there any efforts under way to promote the value and/or communicate the benefits of partici-pating in communities?

    Yes ☐ No ☐

10. Do you have support structures in place to build and sustain communities of practice?

    Yes ☐ No ☐

11. Are individuals recognized and/or rewarded for their participation in communities of practice?

    Yes ☐ No ☐

12. Are there any efforts under way within your organization to integrate communities of practice with knowledge management initiatives?

    Yes ☐ No ☐

13. Have any efforts been made to establish communi-ties that reach out to suppliers, partners, and/or customers?

    Yes ☐ No ☐

Number of "yes" responses _____

SCORE YOURSELF:

0–5 "yes" responses: Although you are no doubt eager to set your course and take those first steps toward your objective, you should be prepared for a significant amount of work to incorporate the necessary concepts and processes. Because many have blazed a trail for you in terms of developing and employing proven approaches, you can take advantage of the lessons they have learned and ensure you're heading in the right direction. Read on to learn more.

6–10 "yes" responses: You are certainly on the right path to building and sustaining communities of practice that will benefit individual community members as well as the organization at large. But there is still much to explore. Your next step should be to identify the areas in which your organization is weakest and focusing your efforts there; you can use the Landmark chapters that follow to help. Once your organization improves in those areas, complete success will be within reach.

11–13 "yes" responses: You are well on your way to demonstrating best practices in the development and nurturing of communities of practice. Your "no" answers will indicate the areas in which your organization needs to improve. Even if you answered "yes" to all of the questions, as you read the following chapters, ask yourself what more you should be doing to strengthen each of the components. The goal is not just to address a particular facet but rather to say you're doing it well enough that its positive impact is felt throughout your organization.

A Communities of Practice Strategy

For years organizations of all types have had informal communities. Hidden deep inside organizational silos, structures, and policies, these communities flourished because the people in them had burning needs or desires to come together to exchange their rich and tacit knowledge. Why? It helped them accomplish their work better, faster, and cheaper. Left alone, these communities may or may not have continued to exist; and they may or may not have leveraged their knowledge or learnings to the enterprise at large.

Hence, as the potential power of these organic forms has emerged, best-practice organizations have made an effort to formalize and strategically develop communities that support the mission and objectives of the business (Figure 1, page 14). Additionally, communities are formally identified and created to help successfully implement other knowledge management approaches such as a knowledge portal or process for transferring best practices.

BEST PRACTICE: THINK LOCALLY, ACT GLOBALLY

Taking a strategic approach to developing communities of practice may be the difference between having dynamic communities that create knowledge and feed its flow or languishing with a few communities adrift in an organizational backwater.

Comparison of Informal and Formal Communities

CoP Elements	Informal	Formal
Sponsorship	• Local • Problem solving—impacts day-to-day work • Shared space and community • Internally establish norms and expectations	• Local to global • Provides systematic charter, framework, and standards • Corporate support teams of KM practitioners • Replicated into the business at different levels
Membership	• Voluntary • People with a passion for the issues • Demand-driven • Subject matter experts recognized by peers	• Virtual teams with changing membership • Membership recruited based upon expertise and responsibility • Focus aligns with business strategy
Roles and Responsibilities	• Informal • Personal networks • Self-providing • Individual content experts • Self-generating	• Formal • Global support structures • Specified roles, such as leader, facilitator, moderator, content manager, validator • Core group of experts

Figure 1

A strategic approach to developing communities of practice allows an organization to take full advantage of its knowledge flow. Communities, if correctly selected and organized, are uniquely positioned to exchange tacit knowledge and determine the usefulness and validity of explicit knowledge by allowing the bearers and creators of knowledge to share, cooperatively create, and use enterprise knowledge. Additionally, the content that the communities create can be used to provide substantial value to the organization.

COMMUNITIES THAT PROVIDE BUSINESS VALUE

As in the case of developing an enterprise KM strategy, an organization must ask itself "What problem are we trying to solve?"

or "What is the business opportunity?" where leveraging knowledge will provide value. The success of communities depends on their integration into both business and KM strategy and, second, integration into structure, daily work, desktop tools and budgets.

How CoPs Provide Business Value

- Identify performance gaps between current practices and best practices in their respective business processes
- Commit to closing gaps with an approach and time frame
- Document successful practices for others to use
- Support and enhance a knowledge-sharing culture

Take the story of a cement manufacturer that needed to stop its various divisions from competing with each other to protect its commodity. With mines and plants nationwide, the organization lost significant funds when plants suspended production because of technical difficulties, but the divisions wouldn't collaborate to solve the problems. A silo mentality and competitive dynamic existed among the plants.

So the company decided to formulate a strategy to create communities that cut across the plants and empowered the plant engineers, maintenance managers, and front-line supervisors. The approach: they built communities around four key performance improvement strategies: productivity, reliability, quality, and safety—all of which affected the bottom line.

Two communities (a productivity community and a reliability community) were launched with process engineers and maintenance managers from several plants. Each group identified sharing opportunities and successful practices as well as created a Web portal to support them.

While the technological solutions supported the sharing of information such as regulations, manuals, and policies and procedures, they did not address the challenges of fostering innovation, building skills, and reusing and leveraging knowledge assets. The members of the communities helped address those challenges. In addition, the senior vice president of operations fostered the communities by 1) engaging the participation of community support across plant managers and 2) participating in the online discussions by offering help and advice.

The immediate benefits realized by the communities were:

- reduction of cycle time to problem resolution,
- elimination of redundant efforts,
- avoidance of repeat mistakes,
- effective learning at the time of need, and
- location and leveraging of expertise and experience.

Expert Advice: Create a Link

The key is to create an ongoing link between the strategy and the formal organization. Schlumberger launched a drilling community to address its greatest and most immediate need—reduce both expenses and the complexity of the drilling process. The formal community that was formed enables Schlumberger engineers to easily access and share lessons learned for future projects.

GETTING STARTED

A community that doesn't understand its reason for existence and its place in achieving organizational goals sets itself up for imminent obsolescence. Many community efforts have failed because of lack of strategic intents and support at the senior level.

A successful strategy starts with ensuring that your KM efforts are playing in the "main tent" in the organization's show. Always playing in the main tent are the most captivating dramas; it's where the competitive threats and opportunities that keep managers awake at night are addressed.

How do you get into the main tent? Involve executives and managers in setting direction for your KM efforts and your community strategy. Their role is to help shape it, sponsor it, fund it, and hold it accountable. Their involvement will ensure that the selected communities will support the business intent, will represent the hottest and most compelling opportunities, and will get the support they need to thrive.

KEY SUCCESS FACTORS

1. Sufficient resources, including money and budgets
2. Cross-functional thought leadership
3. Ongoing facilitation from a central support group
4. IT support
5. Design teams

Sufficient Resources, Including Money and Budgets

Sufficient resources are required for communities to fulfill their intended purpose. Resources include start-up costs, training, facilitation, and leader and member time. Without funding, getting the community off the ground will be difficult. Unless the funding proposal for the community initiative happens to come at the right time in the budgeting cycle to win funding, senior leadership or the community sponsor will have to reallocate time and resources to the effort.

Cross-Functional Thought Leadership

Best-practice organizations report that a cross-functional, high-level group of leaders helps to free up necessary resources. This could be a steering committee, a cross-unit knowledge management task force, or some existing body that provides overall guidance and support, including money and time.

Ongoing Facilitation from a Central Support Group

Formal communities will need an experienced group of KM practitioners to support early efforts. The community membership is usually made up of practitioners and subject matter experts. The design, launch, and deployment of a community often requires skill sets not present inside of the community. A central group engaged to support community meetings and activities requires key skills such as facilitation, change management, project management, communication, and information technology capabilities.

As a community matures and evolves, the central support group will continue to act as internal consultants to the community. In addition, this central body should be devoted to spreading knowledge sharing and community principles and processes throughout the organization and providing tactical support.

IT Support

Information technology costs for basic communication and collaboration tools are typically an enterprise cost and contained in the IT budget. Specialized knowledge sharing and collaboration applications may be included in the central IT budget and allocated to the sponsor or units who benefit from the community.

DESIGN TEAMS

A design team is formed to create the strategic and tactical plans for a successful community. This team will:
- create charters,
- select projects,
- create infrastructure
- design roll-out plans,
- foster support for KM, and
- monitor the results of the CoP.

Through interviews and recommendations from the business process owner, design team members are chosen based on the skills and competencies they bring to community development. The design team serves as an advisory board to the community and a linchpin to the cross-functional thought leadership group. In addition, it follows up throughout the life of the community, monitors its effectiveness, and makes strategic decisions and changes to the community when necessary.

Whether informal or formal, communities have the unique features of being forums for the exchange of tacit knowledge and for determining the quality and usefulness of explicit knowledge. Best-practice organizations continue to provide ongoing evidence that community efforts enhance the implementation of knowledge management and reduce the cycle time to institutionalizing a knowledge-sharing culture.

ROADBLOCKS TO SUCCESS

- Forming a community of practice without considering strategic objectives or identifying the problems the community may help solve
- Failure to integrate the community into the business, the budget, the organizational structure, and the daily work of employees
- Lack of senior-level support
- Weak understanding of CoP's purpose
- Limited financial resources
- Absence of core group of experienced KM practitioners to provide guidance during formative period

CHECK YOUR STATUS

1. Ask yourself, "How can communities work for my organization?"

2. Are there areas where people can solve problems together more quickly by discussing issues and making recommendations?

3. Are there areas where organizational knowledge can be preserved by sharing best practices and lessons learned?

4. Are there areas where skills, relationships, and reputations can be built through the collaboration of practitioners and subject matter experts?

5. Can you identify leaders who believe in the principles of knowledge sharing and will support your effort either financially or by giving it visibility?

6. Do you have an IT infrastructure that can support knowledge sharing or will you have to invest in one?

Types of Communities of Practice

Traditionally the term community implies an informal network: a group of people who communicate with each other because they want to. This definition of community still stands in society, and to some extent in organizations as well.

In studying the various best-practice organizations that served as partners in APQC's *Building and Sustaining Communities of Practice* study, APQC found that a community can be a highly structured group that follows well-defined procedures for sharing practices or a very informal, loose collection of individuals sharing ideas. Some communities are democratic; others are as hierarchical as the organizations in which they reside. Some focus on writing or capturing and organizing practices; others provide a forum for members to discuss and test half-baked ideas.

A community's form is primarily determined by its strategic intent. APQC and Richard McDermott, who served as a subject matter expert for APQC's *Building and Sustaining Communities of Practice* benchmarking study, identified four types of communities based on their strategic intent:

1. helping communities,
2. best-practice communities,

3. knowledge-stewarding communities, and
4. innovation communities.

The type of community is a strong indicator of the knowledge and practices it focuses on, key activities it undertakes, its structure, and its leadership roles. But it should not be assumed that communities serve just one purpose. Many communities have multiple intents, but they usually focus on one. A community's strategic intent requires specific processes and activities to fulfill its purpose. Consider the essential character and business drivers of each community.

HELPING COMMUNITIES

As companies become more team-based and more globally focused, professionals become more isolated from each other. Because their work often involves complex analysis, input from peers is often a critical, though informal, part of their work. Informal and peer-focused helping communities preserve advisory and thinking relationships, even in cross-geographical structures.

Helping communities can be powerful forces in the organization. They provide an outlet for informal discussions concerning individual practices and technical problems. Members build trust among each other to truly admit problems and spontaneously share ideas. These communities focus on connecting members so they can ask for help, learn from the expertise of other members, and understand each other's perspective.

Helping communities exist in practically every organization. They are, however, very small, and members are added by invitation only by other members in the network. As organizations formalize these communities, they create a forum to connect people in separate teams, geography, or business units. With a mechanism in place, the organization allows the members to decide what knowledge to share, how to assess its value, and how to disseminate good ideas to the rest of the community or the whole organization.

A technical community, for example, may post ideas or requests for help on a customized, threaded discussion. The intent to make people-to-people connections is sufficient motivation for scientists and engineers to respond.

Helping communities might also consist of peer groups and networks around a particular issue. For example, some helping communities are focused on diversity, retirement, and relocation— all employee relations issues.

Although all types of communities attempt to reduce costs, helping communities approach the task in a unique way. Because helping communities focus on peer-to-peer relationships, they reduce costs by sharing information and practices developed or used throughout the organization. The organization may also benefit through lower turnover and higher morale.

Due to its informal nature, the majority of knowledge shared within a helping community is typically tacit. Some tacit knowledge may be stored and shared with other members of the community.

BEST-PRACTICE COMMUNITIES

The strategic intent of best-practice communities is to develop, validate, and disseminate proven practices. Whereas helping communities rely on members' knowledge to verify new practices and prompt sharing though help requests and individual insights, best-practice communities have a specific process to verify the effectiveness and benefit of practices and expect members to continuously develop and implement practices. Because structured vetting processes are an inherent attribute of best-practice communities, their success depends on sharing documented practices.

For example, an auto manufacturer's best-practice communities use a process to manage the flow of ideas from an individual insight to a documented, verified, and used practice, when appropriate. The practice is then used at all of its manufacturing plants. Efforts involve:

- a structure for operators and engineers to describe a new practice and its value,

- several reviews in which the knowledge focal point and subject matter experts assess the practice's effectiveness and benefit, and
- a process for ensuring that the practice is distributed and critically reviewed.

Best-practice communities also create cost reductions as well as maintain consistency and quality among dispersed groups by standardizing practices. Through standardized learning, members ensure that lessons are disseminated throughout the organization. Standardization, rather than individual helping relationships, allows a best-practice community to thrive in areas with a fairly concrete application of knowledge. This type of community lends itself to a focus on explicit knowledge. The knowledge is codified and stored so it can be shared in a structured manner.

Organizations also depend on best-practice communities to preserve knowledge in the face of turnover and retirement. Many companies expect large portions of their experienced, knowledgeable work forces to retire in the next decade. Best-practice communities provide a means to capture some of that valuable knowledge and codify it to pass on.

KNOWLEDGE-STEWARDING COMMUNITIES

Although most companies realize the importance of cost savings, consistency, and utilizing technology, an ultimate accomplishment for any organization is to have a group of individuals that will organize, develop, and disseminate the organization's knowledge in their area of expertise. A knowledge-stewarding community does just that. Like the aforementioned communities, knowledge-stewarding communities host forums for members to connect, develop, and verify practices, but the main intent of these communities is to organize, upgrade, and distribute the knowledge their members use on a day-to-day basis.

Organizations need standard arrangements for their front-line staffs to access knowledge that allows them to remain competitive, as well as reorganize, merge, or change roles in the marketplace. Knowledge-stewarding communities arrange knowledge—the core material for their daily responsibilities—to be refined, verified, and updated.

Many consulting companies follow this model to acquire a better position in the market. For example, Cap Gemini Ernst & Young estimates having 1.2 million documents in its general, unfiltered repositories; 875,000 documents in discussion databases; and 50,000 documents in topical kits for consultant use. The primary focus of the firm's 150 communities is to manage that content.

Cap Gemini Ernst & Young believes that most new ideas originate informally during the course of a project, especially within project materials that members prepare. Those ideas need to be located, organized, and distributed. To do so, Cap Gemini Ernst & Young tasks the knowledge-stewarding community with organizing documents, presentations, data, proposals, and approaches. Its responsibilities extend to creating relationships among community members, sharing ideas, increasing productivity, and accommodating customer needs.

INNOVATION COMMUNITIES

As its name indicates, innovation communities foster unexpected, innovative ideas and practices. Although all communities encourage members to create and share new practices, innovation communities intentionally cross boundaries and bring together members with different perspectives to promote an inventive atmosphere.

Organizations find such communities extremely helpful when they have no medium to connect distinct areas of innovation. New ideas and quickly changing knowledge are circulated more effectively through the organization, even if they are not documented, verified, or tested.

Innovation communities also are helpful when faced with a fast-changing marketplace. For example, an innovation community can collect and analyze technology trends, and community members can ask people on other projects about emerging technologies. Because most technology developments occur outside an organization, such a community can find outside contacts. A community concerned with emerging trends may also set an expiration date on disseminated ideas and information.

DaimlerChrysler has an innovation community that connects 240 dispersed experts to assess new directions in designing cars. Members include employees from business and functional units as well as from research and engineering. This is a medium for their innovative ideas to be realized in new or improved products. In addition to introducing new products, members are expected by the company's KM board and research and technology department to complete projects successfully, improve job performance, and provide growth opportunities for members. This formalized community is unique in that it allows members to breach normal reporting relationships by reaching out to various functions and positions.

In a separate example concerning a telecommunications company, engineers and scientists were often assigned to different platform teams but worked with the same technology. Personal networks provided limited opportunities to discuss emerging technologies, so innovation communities were formalized across teams.

Hewlett-Packard Consulting's business analysts are organized by industry. But to develop innovative ideas, they formed a community that crosses industry lines to take advantage of their differences in perspective and bring ideas from different companies and industries on each business case. This allows them to analyze clients' business processes and recommend innovative redesigns using information technology.

By identifying the strategic intent and thus the type of community appropriate for the organization, the design process designs itself. The four community types have distinctive activities, structures, and relationships within the community. The type also will have a significant affect on how communities are supported and integrated into the organization.

ESSENTIAL ROLES

Organizations' increasing reliance on communities is evident from their integration into the budgeting and planning process. Consequently, communities have assumed a more formal role.

The roles of members also are formalizing. Community members often are held accountable for producing and stewarding knowledge, saving time and money, and assuming an influential standing in the organization. Roles differ according to strategic intent and host organization, but the roles that are required for the successful initiation of a formal community are:

1. **Sponsor**—A community sponsor, who can be a high-level executive or a mid-level manager, supports the community through funding, promotion, or tapping human resources.
2. **Leader**—As the architect of the community, the leader passionately develops the topic or specialty area. Responsibilities involve ensuring newly acquired knowledge is used to the advantage of the organization. In small communities, the sponsor can also be the leader.
3. **Member**—Obviously, this is the most common role in a community. The members' responsibility is to carry out the strategic intent by sowing personal input and taking advantage of the community's harvest. Involvement may be required in certain organizations and departments, or it may be a voluntary activity.

The most critical success factor for a community is the leader's skills and background. A leader's responsibilities vary among communities types:

- **Helping communities**—Leaders unite potential members, identify collaborative projects, and manage information and documents.
- **Best-practice communities**—Leaders manage the transformation of ideas into verified, dispersed practices.

- **Knowledge-stewarding communities**—Leaders remove organizational barriers to knowledge and keep the community focused on organizational objectives.
- **Innovation communities**—Leaders find a balance between letting the community grow on its own and steering the community in the strategic direction of the company.

Additional roles such as those of IT specialists, subject matter experts, content managers, and librarians also are valuable. The more complex the strategic intent of the community, the more roles that are required.

Starting and Sustaining Communities of Practice

S trategically, communities reflect their organizations, but they develop and operate quite differently. Membership in a community is typically voluntary and develops naturally. Once an organization identifies naturally occurring, informal networks, it can apply the networks' organic characteristics to form communities within the traditional mechanisms of an organizational structure. Consequently, the networks take on formal checks and balances that reflect the organization.

However, a community's operation cannot be confused with team projects. Whereas teams focus on an achievable goal, such as bringing a new product to market, communities focus on sharing ideas and insights. Of course, teams often share ideas and learn together, and communities often spawn project teams. But communities generally fill in the gaps between organizational units.

The challenge lies in maintaining a flexible, voluntary tone while establishing support structures to institutionalize the network. Successful communities rely on passion, leadership, influence, integration, and organizational relevance. This chapter focuses on incorporating those qualities into community development. This strong foundation sustains the community through its evolution.

STARTING COMMUNITIES

Starting a community involves the 10 following steps:

1. Create a business case for community development.
2. Find community leaders and champions.
3. Define the scope of the community.
4. Design the community's core activities and structure.
5. Recruit and engage community members.
6. Align with the culture.
7. Design community roles.
8. Develop a support structure.
9. Launch the community.
10. Implement appropriate information technology.

The need for flexibility as well as institutional strength can be addressed at each step. Those steps that involve senior management involvement are addressed here.

Find Community Leaders

Voluntary participation necessitates passionate and inspirational leaders to maintain active membership numbers. Therefore, finding community leaders and champions is critical to community development. Leaders are typically engaged through invitation, election, or an evident conviction to the topic. Examples follow for each recruitment approach.

- **DaimlerChrysler** invites people considered good leaders to assume leadership. The executive vice president reviews potential community coordinators based on their skills in leadership, networking, organizational knowledge, current community activity, access to management, and technical expertise.

- A **Schlumberger** senior vice president invited all employees to nominate themselves for community leadership positions. His invitation gave the election process legitimacy. Candidates campaigned by describing why they would make good leaders, and some of these positions were hotly debated.

- **The World Bank** allowed leaders to naturally emerge by announcing that it had resources to support communities. Interested employees submitted proposals for various topics. Those whose proposals were accepted became the de facto leaders of the community.

Define the Scope of a Community

Defining the scope of a community is one of the most challenging steps. The scope must involve a prevalent, enduring issue to both the organization and community members. The best definition of a community's scope comes from community leaders. They understand the potential for a focus area and push that focus to the cutting edge. The scope is defined through a handful of approaches.

The overall work process is a common approach to defining the scope. By segmenting the components of a process, organizations can pinpoint focal points for communities. This approach works well for organizations with concrete processes, such as DaimlerChrysler. Although its platforms differ, certain engineered components, such as wiper engineering or final assembly, are common to all platforms. This approach connects communities to members' day-to-day responsibilities.

Other organizations connect the scope to key disciplines, such as structural engineering or cartography. Communities can be organized by disciplines as small as sci-fi video games and as large as information technology. People who have practiced a discipline for years, especially a scientific one, are particularly useful in cross-functional communities.

Companies can also define the scope of communities by focusing on strategic business needs or opportunities. When the cube farm seems like fields of isolated and hidden crops, a community can harvest basic knowledge that simply needs to be shared. Members who have similar responsibilities or concerns can use the community forum to establish widespread knowledge. If collective knowledge already exists, then gains originate from new topics and external insights.

Whichever defining approach is chosen needs boundaries. Will members come from one group or from different business units and levels of the organization? Will there be special interest groups within a discipline? By building on natural, boundary-crossing networks, organizations can balance conflicting needs. An expansive topic may not maintain members' interest, but a narrow topic may prohibit fresh ideas and insights, which will also alienate members.

Consequently, boundaries are often set by breaking an overall topic into several smaller topics or focus areas. Each subdivided topic is clearly related to the overall scope, but day-to-day interaction is limited to the subdivided-topic level.

Align With the Culture

Knowledge sharing is a voluntary activity. If an organization's culture does not embrace sharing knowledge, communities are useless. If sharing ideas and insights is less pressing than team and individual responsibilities, then community participation, even when valuable, is eclipsed by more individual goals. Instead of forcing employees to participate, successful organizations align the initiative with a receptive culture.

To create a receptive culture, employees must learn how knowledge sharing can solve business problems or enhance business opportunities. Organizations ensure this by aligning knowledge sharing with supported, core values and by introducing all necessary support systems and structures. Some organizations emphasize the importance of knowledge sharing by incorporating it into the budget. As managers and peers encourage knowledge sharing, a more receptive culture forms using existing networks.

A developing community can then parallel its organization's structure. The community structures at DaimlerChrysler and Ford are remarkably similar to their organizational structures, despite essentially voluntary community participation and contribution. Although members of Ford's Best Practice Replication group aren't forced to adopt practices developed in other plants, members feel it would be foolish not to take advantage of the opportunity. DaimlerChrysler estimates that 30 percent of the success of its knowledge management efforts can be attributed to the culture of the organization (only 10 percent to 20 percent to the use of technology).

Recruit and Engage Community Members

Many companies find that drawing on employees' existing interests is the most effective way to recruit and engage community members. For instance, DaimlerChrysler reunited engineers who had worked together before the organization divided into platform teams. Xerox's communities were institutionalized when developers noticed that repair employees consulted each other about difficult repair issues. A formal structure allowed repair employees to reach a community of peers beyond their geographical location.

After gauging existing interests, successful organizations build a support structure through:
* intrinsic motivation,
* relevance,
* professional development, and
* recognition and rewards.

Intrinsic Motivation

Meaningful topics elicit passionate participation. Joining a community may be based on perceived interest and expected value; maintaining membership is a result of becoming emotionally connected to the community, and connecting with others who share similar passion is rewarding in itself. Members derive a sense of satisfaction from contributing to something larger than themselves or connecting with others.

When Schlumberger's communities were launched in 1998, employees were invited to register their interests and indicate to which community they wished to belong. Within two months, more than 2,700 Schlumberger employees were registered members of various communities. These communities provide a sense of identity for employees.

At the World Bank, the most successful communities allowed staff members to select the issues. The organization discovered that unless the members of the thematic group are already passionate about the topic area during development, the thematic group will not have the energy to sustain itself.

Relevance

Membership also is a chance to perfect one's craft; it's an opportunity to learn new tools, techniques, and approaches. Employees are often more than willing to participate in communities that are relevant to their day-to-day responsibilities. Many people receive direct benefits from participating in a community, such as assistance with a problem, access to new ideas or technology, or time saved looking for information. When important information is dispersed in communities, membership flourishes. At Cap Gemini Ernst & Young, community participation is critical for consultants. Communities provide access to the accumulated knowledge of peers, which is an invaluable resource during client engagements. Access to this information enables a consultant to effectively sell business with less effort.

Professional Development

Many companies have taken steps to institutionalize community participation by incorporating it into employees' performance appraisal. Among companies APQC has studied, several built knowledge sharing into the performance appraisal process. But they saw these as attempts to encourage and support natural knowledge sharing, not as attempts to motivate it from outside. This reflects the organic nature of the community by encouraging a natural phenomenon.

Employees at DaimlerChrysler are encouraged to participate in tech clubs for professional development. DaimlerChrysler's annual review for engineers cites sharing knowledge as a key behavior, and the easiest way for employees to excel on this rating is through community participation. No employee can receive a maximum bonus or salary increase without fulfilling this requirement.

Recognition and Rewards

Although passion and relevance are arguably more important in engaging members, recognition and rewards can reinforce industrious behavior. Rewards (such as bonuses and gifts) and explicit recognition (such as peer acknowledgment, letters from senior managers, and award luncheons) can be costly. But some organizations contend that recognizing and rewarding community members emphasize the importance of knowledge management to the entire organization.

Launch The Community

The challenge of launching a community can be alleviated by a process approach. APQC has found examples from several successful companies of systematic, formal approaches to community launches. One company uses a 63-step process that involves identifying topics, roles, senior sponsorship, and measures. Another company launched its communities in a two-day workshop. Community leaders selected from outside models and made a process to determine the scope, membership guidelines, goals, protocol, and support structure. Participants reviewed their decisions with community members.

SUSTAINING COMMUNITIES OVER TIME

Given the appropriate flexibility and institutionalization during the initial stages, a maturing community will inevitably evolve. New members will introduce fresh insights and new ideas. Meanwhile, technology will advance, practices will improve or be replaced, original members will get pulled away, and demands from the organization will change. Such adjustments can rejuvenate or annihilate a community. But even active communities will fluctuate in productivity as they respond to the changes in their environment, organization, scope, and available technology.

A strong indicator of long-term viability is a community's leadership. Many companies do not provide as much support to mature communities as to new ones, but they tend to provide some support by coaching community leaders. By uniting members, examining practices, and representing the member base, community leaders are in a highly visible position. The most involved leaders have the most vibrant communities.

At Ford, community leaders generate and maintain interest by reviewing activity levels within a community and encouraging its members. In Schlumberger's communities, leaders act as social directors, knowledge managers, external contacts or liaisons, and links between the community and management. At Cap Gemini Ernst & Young, the community leader drives content creation and deployment. He or she also is responsible for driving the community toward increasing revenues in their area of expertise and enhancing profits. The community leader is the link to the firm's knowledge assets, other communities, support groups, practices, knowledge repositories, and external resources.

Communities with strong leadership may gain a stronger voice in the organization. For example, the technical communities at one best-practice company formed primarily for peers to help each other. But as they matured, the leaders asked for a stronger advisory role in influencing the technical strategy of the company.

Encourage Evolution

Fluctuating participation and productivity can be disconcerting for community leaders and members. A topic may run its course, members may become diverted, and the community may need to refocus or dissolve. It is the community leaders' responsibility to rejuvenate activity levels, with the support of the organization's leaders.

First, an organization can assess the progress of its communities and coach community leaders based on findings. An accurate assessment includes interviews with community leaders and members about activities, goals, accomplishments, and enrichment opportunities. Second, organizations can organize renewal workshops to reevaluate communities' direction or constitution, structure, and processes. Third, organizations can set up a structure to allow leaders from different communities to share ideas and experiences that allow them to reinvigorate their own communities. A redefined focus can then enable community leaders to increase membership or possibly influence business strategy.

Institutionalize Communities

Institutionalizing communities ensures the networks have the support and tools to excel, even when faced with challenges and growing pains. It also ensures that each community's scope and strategy are parallel with the overall strategy of the organization.

APQC found four key steps to institutionalizing communities without depriving them of their flexibility or organic characteristics.

1. **Simply make employees more aware of communities.** For example, employees at one company have access to community activities through their computers. On the company intranet, the news center provides daily updates from around the world and around the company. And consultants can access a global database of employee information by last name, country, or expertise. External community subject matter experts also are listed. Employees are equipped to ship knowledge around the world from the intranet with relative ease.

2. **Create a mechanism to influence business strategy.** As communities harness their members' knowledge, the organization can apply it to other activities, such as field activities or technology purchases. At some best-practice companies, institutionalized communities are highly influential. For example, communities at one company are structured to influence the organization and consequently create accountability within the membership base. Each community is responsible for reporting its developments to its

subdivided groups and supervisory groups. This ensures that the communities operate strategically.

3. **Allow employees time to participate.** When pressing issues arise, members may overlook the long-term benefits of community participation. Regular community events can reinforce participation as an everyday responsibility. At one best-practice company, a community support team notifies members every week of new practices. The approach is so popular that members call to determine the cause when a message is late.

4. **Incorporate community needs into routine budgeting and planning.** This can be aligned with an annual review of the communities' progress. For instance, one company annually reviews community topics, assesses their strategic importance, and determines their annual budget. Financial needs involve a part-time or full-time community leader as well as the time commitment of community members. This ensures that communities are relevant to current strategic business objectives, visibly endorsed by senior management, and seen by first-line supervisors and others as genuinely important.

KEY LESSONS FOR STARTING AND SUSTAINING COMMUNITIES

The central focus through all of the steps and practices introduced in this chapter is balancing flexibility with structure and support. Supporting communities through their development is a delicate balance between keeping them alive and avoiding dependence on the support team. Other lessons include the following:

• Create a receptive culture where communities will thrive.
• Define the scope narrowly enough so that people are engaged but broadly enough to accept new ideas and interests.
• The key figure is the community leader. If an organization selects an able and enthusiastic community leader, that person will carry out the rest of the process.

- Consider the relevancy of community topics to members' day-to-day responsibilities.
- Rely on members' passion for the topic by making membership voluntary.
- Allow flexibility so that the community can adapt its scope to the changing needs of the organization.
- Intrinsic rewards and recognition are more important than extrinsic rewards for sustaining participation.
- Reward productive communities with a seat at the decision-making table. Communities with a clearly defined scope, lightly supported with coaching and workshops, are helpful in decisions regarding their domain.

Support Structures

A core group of passionate community members usually drives the activity and participation level of a community. When those advocates move on or their passion wanes, the community often dies. But communities don't have to fold. With support from multiple levels of the organizational hierarchy, struggling communities can break into smaller communities or change direction. By creating support structures that can help and direct communities, companies have enabled communities to be a sustainable part of the organizational structure and to contribute positively to the bottom line of the company.

This chapter focuses on the responsibilities of a support group and major models for support.

SUPPORT GROUP RESPONSIBILITIES

A formal or expansive hierarchy has little function in a community of practice. An autocratic approach stifles the creativity and sense of individuality that originates from networks of peers. Consequently, management takes on a role more supportive than supervisory in the development of communities of practice. Support groups provide direction, processes, and resources for each community type.

The support group's place in the organizational hierarchy determines the relationship and the degree to which the communities tie into the overall organization structure, as well as their connection to the senior management team. The amount of involvement from senior management correlates to the amount of influence a community may exercise. Support can be organized at a corporate or functional level (sometimes both).

At a corporate level, a support group can be an overarching knowledge management steering team, community, or board. The roles may include a sponsor, an owner, a leader, or a team of managers whose function is to approve funding, monitor progress, and ensure that the community goals are aligned with the strategic goals of the company.

At a functional level, support is usually provided by a product group, a division/business unit, or an IT organization. Support groups at a functional level support facilitation, coordinate meetings and networking sessions, set priorities, provide subject matter expertise, manage content, and/or act as liaisons between the communities and senior management.

FOUR MODELS

Although communities are free-flowing and cross functional boundaries, their support structures tend to reflect the formal structure of the overall organization. Consequently, the community is viewed as a legitimate part of the organization, with the benefits of funding.

APQC has found four models for support: board support model, community of leaders support model, central staff support model, and functional-level support model. Several hybrids of these models are also in practice. They are defined by the amount and kind of support required.

The Board Support Model

The board support model is applicable to organizations developing helping communities. In this model, a board guides the direction and the outcomes of the community. However, in helping communities that are peer driven and democratic, the support organization provides fewer resources and is there only in case the community needs it.

APQC found a demonstrative example of the board support model at the World Bank. Support groups existed at levels throughout the organization. At the corporate level, a knowledge-sharing support group coordinates the communities across the Bank. Their support extends to:

- providing strategic leadership;
- developing communities;
- working with departments such as IT, research, and evaluation;
- monitoring how processes are standardized;
- monitoring member activities;
- soliciting external ideas; and
- training the staff.

Sector boards also contribute to community development. Twenty sectors span six geographical regions, and a sector board is made up of directors from each region. Sector boards determine the overall sector strategy, monitor knowledge sharing, update the skills and competencies of staff members, and budget for each community based on work program agreements that are in line with the sector strategy. Consequently, sector priorities reflect community priorities.

Typically, communities have three to five co-leaders who assume part-time responsibility for the communities. A junior facilitator may be employed to organize meetings, respond to inquiries, maintain Web sites, and write and distribute newsletters.

All networks have advisory services (some at the network level, others at the sector level) that provide answers to questions, often obtaining the answers from community members. Annual Sector Weeks, organized by the corporate KM group, are the principal tool for incorporating sectors and providing connectivity among the World Bank's communities of practice.

The Community of Leaders Support Model

The community of leaders support model is more interactive at the intermediate levels of support provided for communities. The leader from each community in a specialty area is part of a leaders community that acts as the liaison between the communities and management.

This structure is used at DaimlerChrysler. Communities are organized by specialty areas, which are further divided into groups by subspecialty. The leaders of the specialty area communities, or tech clubs, are part of a community called executive tech clubs. The executive tech clubs define the priorities and set goals for the tech clubs, and they also disseminate information to the executive vice presidents and other senior leaders. The group acts as a liaison between the engineers and management, which allows both groups to focus their attention on their respective specialties.

Each tech club at DaimlerChrysler is relied upon as a subject matter expert for the organization. The experts therefore steward the knowledge in their area of expertise and influence product decisions.

A support group called the KM Forum ensures consistency among KM programs across DaimlerChrysler; it provides start-up kits for groups that want to develop communities. The start-up kits include templates for agendas, information on conducting meetings, and a description of roles and responsibilities.

The Central Staff Support Model

The central staff support model represents a knowledge management initiative that is not necessarily tied into an overarching corporate KM program. This does not imply that the KM initiative is not aligned with the strategic goals of the organization, just that there is no formal corporate KM program.

In this model, communities are informal; the reporting structure and the accountability associated with implementing best practices from a community are not. The support group provides technology and training and monitors the activity of the community. The key roles in this support model are those of community administrator and community leader.

This model reflects the community structure at Ford, whose Best-Practice Replication community is tied structurally to day-to-day management. The executive sponsor performs the traditional responsibilities of gaining budget approval and support. The support group is part of the process leadership function, which is responsible for leveraging technology to improve work processes. The end goal is to gather best-practice information on successful processes and to disseminate them for reuse in other plants.

Every Ford employee on the plant floor is considered a community member. The employees submit suggestions for process or machine improvements for their plant floors to their community leader, referred to as the focal point. The focal point submits the idea to the community administrator, a subject matter expert who validates it. Once a practice has been validated, it is sent out to all the plants for implementation. If a practice is not implemented at a certain plant, the supervisors of that plant have to explain why implementation did not take place.

The Functional-Level Support Model

The functional-level support model involves two support groups. One is an internal board that oversees a strategic KM or community objective defined by senior management. Second is the community support group that builds and sustains communities in a functional area.

The model also involves either a formal KM group or a community of KM champions at the corporate level. The group ensures that

KM is consistently deployed across the organization. By sharing knowledge of community activities, redundancy is avoided and the reuse of information increases.

Xerox's Corporate Engineering Center (CEC) communities are supported in this manner. The CEC supports, leads, or facilitates communities such as software process improvement and hardware solutions development because the outputs of these communities decreases time-to-market results. The CEC organizes meetings, sets the agenda, selects speakers, stewards the Web site, and designs the charter. This role is most helpful in developing communities because more mature communities are self-sustaining.

KEY LESSONS FOR SUPPORT STRUCTURES

Support structures for communities of practice are designed to align with the organization's structure so that communities' reporting hierarchy reflects traditional functional units, with comparable levels of accountability according to their mission, goals, and available resources.

Strong support structures at the corporate level with minimal functional-level support usually indicate the maturity of a community. At this stage community participation is completely integrated into a member's workday. On the other hand, strong support at the functional level may imply a commitment from management to communities; if members have their hands full with day-to-day responsibilities, they may need extra help in validating information, coordinating meetings, and avoiding redundancy.

The four models for supporting communities reflect different types of communities, with different intents. The appropriate model also is determined by the organizational structure and the communities' degree of maturity.

Funding Models for Communities

Information technology budgets for knowledge management will usually not cover the costs of building communities of practice. IT budgets typically include monies for communities' basic communication, collaboration tools, and applications needs, but APQC's research shows that in order to be successful, an organization must provide for start-up costs, training, facilitation, and leader and member time to ensure a community can reach its full potential.

FUNDING AND THE BUSINESS CASE

In examining best-practice organizations, APQC identified five stages common to successful knowledge management implementation (Figure 2, page 48). Funding and budget allocation for KM varies across the five stages, moving from indirect, informal funding in the early stages, through increased centralized budgeting, to a realignment of resources whereby business units take up more of the budget load.

Initial funding for communities of practice will typically occur in Stage 3 during the design and launch of KM initiatives (Figure 3, page 49). Once the organization has identified its KM strategy in Stage 2, pilot projects will be identified to test KM principles and

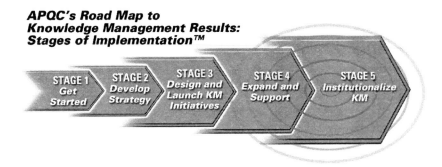

Figure 2

build support for larger-scale efforts. It is in Stage 3 that most organizations undertake the building of communities of practice and must then address the funding issues. Our research points to a mixed funding approach at this stage by which the business unit funds the resources required to design and roll out the CoP, while supporting resources may be provided from central budgets or out of a KM program office.

Budgets Across the Stages of KM Implementation

Best-practice organizations have reported that a cross-functional, high-level KM task force or central oversight group helps to free up these resources. This group may be a steering committee, a cross-unit KM task force, or some existing body that provides overall guidance and support, including money and time.

Start-up and implementation costs vary widely. Fifty-six percent of those organizations studied by APQC and deemed to have advanced KM programs in place have spent more than $1 million on costs associated with Stages 1 through 3, whereas about half of the organizations in Stages 1 and 2 have spent less than $100,000. Annual maintenance requires at least the same level of investment. Within APQC's KM consortia, many organizations' leaders are of the opinion that their KM budgets will increase in the future.

KM Budgets Across the Stages of KM Implementation

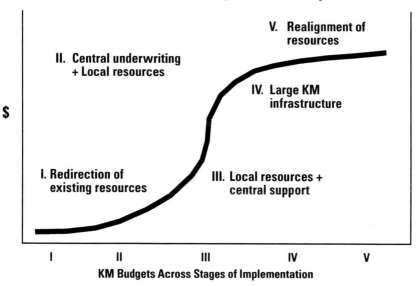

KM Budgets Across Stages of Implementation

Figure 3

Money is one hurdle; the other is to find or create a group of experienced KM practitioners and free up enough of their time to support a community of practice initiative. The people supporting CoPs need key skills relating to facilitation, change management, project management, communication, and information technology (for best-practice repositories and Web sites). The early champions and core KM team are typically the pioneers from which this group is started and grown. Figure 4, page 50, lists some of the categories of resources needed to design and launch the community.

KEY LESSONS FOR FUNDING MODELS
- Some central funding and support helps business units to develop communities and can reinforce cross-organizational knowledge-sharing behavior.
- During start-up, participants' time is the main cost in a community.

People Costs	Process Costs	Technology Costs
CoP Leader(s)	Taxonomy development	Databases
Meeting/planning facilitators	Standards development	Collaboration tools
Content managers	Rewards and recognition	Expert locator/yellow pages
Best practice/content validation	Metrics and reporting	System integration
	Communication	
	Training	
	Content validation	

Figure 4

- As the community matures, business units tend to take on more and more of the cost.
- Cross-functional support from corporate groups such as IT and HR is critical to developing and sustaining the community system.

Information Technology and Content Management

K nowledge management initiatives typically use some form of information technology to connect people with people and people to information and knowledge. APQC has monitored the importance of information technology at best-practice organizations since 1995. IT consistently has been recognized not as the primary driver of but an essential enabler to effective knowledge sharing. What is the difference? Organizations that build technology tools with the assumption that they will improve knowledge sharing by themselves have missed the boat. However, every best-practice organization has unlocked the power of its people's knowledge by enabling employees with IT tools that make finding, sharing, and using information easier and more effective. So KM practitioners will benefit from assessing their communities' IT and content management needs early in the life cycle of the community.

DEVELOPMENTS IN KM AND INFORMATION TECHNOLOGY

As technology has evolved, so has the perception of its role in knowledge management. In the mid-1990s, knowledge-sharing IT systems, based around CD-ROM and database technologies, required a significant investment of time and money. The late 1990s led to a focus on Internet- and intranet-based strategies, but investment amounts were still considerable. As more organizations developed a presence on the Internet, created or bought portal tools, and moved to standardized desktop computing platforms, incredible knowledge-sharing opportunities emerged.

Due to this existing and growing connectivity, many organizations then shifted their knowledge management focus from wires and bytes to the social aspects of KM. In fact, in APQC's *Successfully Implementing Knowledge Management* study, conducted in 2000, this shift from IT to a focus on the social aspects of KM was very apparent. Organizations began to focus on the cultural drivers behind sharing knowledge, such as face-to-face meetings, virtual chat rooms, and building trust through personal communication. Existing technology tools were enhanced or modified to represent the social realities of the organization, not to show the latest and greatest functionality.

In the early part of the 21st century, technology advances are becoming more and more affordable for the majority of organizations. Additionally, many companies have begun capitalizing on existing desktop tools they already possess, such as MS Outlook and Lotus Notes. Interestingly, best-practice organizations indicated that e-mail remains the most frequently used tool for knowledge sharing because of its relative ubiquity, speed, and personal nature. Because of this fact, and the danger that lies in having an organization's knowledge tied up on the hard drives and e-mail folders of its employees, software companies are now developing e-mail mining programs that discover important knowledge that should be shared. As with any technology, however, people need to develop processes to capitalize on these tools and promote sensible use.

APQC has found, through nine consortium studies and extensive client work, that no technology platform can entirely supplant the need for frequent face-to-face interaction (either formal and informal). This face-to-face interaction is an excellent forum for communities to share tacit, undocumented knowledge. The best knowledge-sharing organizations combine useful technology with rich personal interactions to find, validate, share, and use knowledge to enhance their business results.

CONTENT MANAGEMENT

Content management, which involves the identification, collection, and management of content within an organization, is a crucial element of IT and KM initiatives. KM leaders faced with defining the life cycle of content, gathering an inventory of existing content, selecting a taxonomy, and creating a content validation system can address such issues through building an effective content management system. APQC's research and experience shows that content management quickly becomes a limiting factor in any knowledge management effort. Get your hands around it early and you will save time and heartache down the road.

A content management system should provide standard approaches for content ownership, use, storage, and classification. Without it, important documents and knowledge can be lost or buried, online data can become stale, and sharing will decline because people will not find what they need.

APQC researched several examples of working content management systems in its eighth KM research consortium, *Managing Content and Knowledge* (2001). For instance, one best-practice organization provides centrally funded content managers, who are former practitioners from a community of practice and are well versed in the nature of community knowledge. They teach community members how to place taxonomic coordinates (metadata or key words) on a document so it can be located easily. These content managers also train authors to write abstracts that colleagues can quickly review for applicability. Consequently, members can create a template, work plan, or a white paper and disseminate it to the entire community with relative ease.

Another approach to content management is to manage the information purchased externally and make it available to communities. Oftentimes, employees repeatedly purchase the same content from external information providers, apparently unaware that the content is available internally. This approach allows an organization to gather subscriptions under one umbrella by centralizing purchasing and redistribution of all external content. One best-practice company discovered significant savings by using this approach and found that its access to information increased.

There are a growing number of technology vendors that sell content management solutions in the marketplace. Many of these vendors sell software packages and consulting services that help organizations move from the genesis of content management to a full-blown solution via taxonomies, metadata, workflow, search capabilities, and data mining. As with many other areas of information technology, these solutions differ in quality and focus, so researching the options thoroughly before making a decision is important. With that in mind, APQC's *Managing Content and Knowledge* study included a content management vendor assessment aimed at helping organizations determine which provider might be right for their needs, what questions to ask, and what resources to call on as they develop an effective knowledge and content management initiative.

KEY LESSONS

- Although more affordable for most organizations, IT applications are still complex and require resources.
- Remember that the people and processes, not IT, need to drive your communities of practice. IT tools should enable easier, more effective sharing.
- Whereas collaborative tools and e-mail tremendously enrich opportunities to communicate, face-to-face interaction is still the most effective medium for community work. One potential setback may be attention and time overload from the variety of media.

- Community members need to be able to communicate in real time rather than download information or communicate in an asynchronous mode. Collaborative software enables such communication.
- IT tools should be designed around the community's needs, not vice versa.
- Content management must be addressed early in the community life cycle. Content quickly becomes the limiting factor for most communities.
- There are a variety of technology vendors in the marketplace with robust solutions. Use APQC's Content Management Vendor Assessment or the Internet to research which opportunities will work best for your organization.

Measuring the Impact of Communities

The prevalence of cost centers and operations managers focused solely on billable time indicates the importance organizations place on accounting for and measuring how an employee's time is spent. As communities become institutionalized and exercise influence, they are integrated into day-to-day responsibilities and consequently require more of people's time and energy. That increased time must be justified; consequently, the existence of the community must be justified through measurement.

Yet measurement is not entirely a bottom-line pretense to justify funding. Rather, measurement has the power to focus attention on desired behaviors and results. Well-designed measurement systems beget successful knowledge management initiatives.

WHAT CAN YOU MEASURE?

How communities are measured should reflect strategic intent, tactical design, and degree of maturity. There is no single, perfect measure of community success because the definition of success varies from organization to organization, and often community to community.

Assessment is beneficial to both developing and mature communities of practice. Communities in uncharted territory need objec-

---

Measurement Tips

- Focus on the critical few measures
- Aim for balance and accuracy
- Don't create measurement schemes that are more trouble than they are worth

---

tive indicators of progress and success in operations. To ensure ongoing support from the organization, developing communities can act strategically by using continuous assessments as an early-warning system for correction. Mature communities can use measures to underscore the goals of knowledge management, drive and reinforce knowledge-sharing behavior, assess progress, and possibly reassess direction.

APQC has identified two frameworks to measure the impact of a community of practice. The first framework assesses the health of the organization. With a focus on the tactical operations of a community, information regarding effectiveness or value is often more strategic. The second framework assesses the effectiveness of the community. To accurately assess the status of communities, having information from both frameworks is essential.

Community Health

This framework for continuous assessment provides community leaders with information regarding community activity. Developing communities need to assess their structure and define community goals in the early planning stages. A wide variety of output measures will highlight links to organization strategy and gauge the capacity for knowledge to flow. As the community matures, assessment will continue to involve content management system use, participation levels, and the number of problems solved by the community. But this framework does not describe the value that the community provides to the organization.

Community Effectiveness

Most organizations do not assess the value of communities from the outset. Instead, communities have a chance to develop and grow; then the organization begins to measure its contributions. The second measurement framework is community effectiveness, which is the value that a community provides to an organization, such as reduced cycle time, increased customer savings, repeat business, and reduced cost of doing business.

An organization may measure the progress of the community toward its goals. Or an organization may measure the value that communities provide by collecting stories and anecdotes from community organizers, members, and leaders. Through storytelling activities. Community members and leaders are given the opportunity to trace the value of community participation to a higher level of efficiency in their everyday work. Consequently, this framework more easily lends itself to qualitative measures. In the early stages of a community, capturing and sharing success stories—big or small— is key.

EXAMPLES OF MEASUREMENT SYSTEMS
DaimlerChrysler

DaimlerChrysler developed three measures to register successful communities.

1. **Output measures**—These quantitative measures report how many people attend a meeting, how many hits a Web site receives, and how many contributions are made to knowledge management tools. Alone, output measures do not reveal if the community is supporting the company's business goals.
2. **Link to business outcomes**—Communities must demonstrate how they support business goals. This link often is not direct or mathematical in nature. Reduced cycle time in processing loan

applications creates satisfied customers in Chrysler financial services, while a new rust-resistant material may help sustain a lasting competitive advantage. A global view of operations and goals is required to understand the link between the community activity and the organizational goals.

3. **Community health**—Community health focuses on measuring how well a community operates. Leaders track member satisfaction, activity levels, enhanced reputation of the organization, impact on traditional business metrics, and contribution to business goals. Data is gathered from a variety of sources including surveys of community members, interviews with leaders and members, and business results.

Separately, these three measures will not reveal the effectiveness or health of a community. But in blending the three types of measures together, DaimlerChrysler can assess its communities' health, activity, and contribution toward business goals.

Ford

Ford continuously assesses its communities from the development stage, at which point measures are deliberately simple. Ford has developed a measurement application with many built-in reporting features. This application can segment information by community. Measures range from a macro-level, general summary to extremely detailed reports showing all feedback and comments, which are analyzed by the core groups and mined for strategy and trends. Mature communities, such as the final area business plan, use a complicated methodology to monitor time spent by members of the community. Senior management then sees the conversion to money.

Ford's Process Leadership Team measures value, safety, quality, timing, throughput, and cost reduction, but not ROI. Instead, the value of the implemented best practices is tracked. Costs associated with applying best practices to the plant level require approval, but do not require a detailed ROI calculation.

As a result of continuous assessment, Ford attributes approximately $1 billion of value added to the company from its Best-Practice Replication program and rapid application process improvement deployment. The company cites more than 5,000 replications a year, $1.25 billion of projected value, $850 million of actual value added to the company (of the 2,800-plus high-value practices), and revenue from licensing the best-practice replication process.

World Bank

Although the World Bank does not believe it is possible to establish an ROI for knowledge management, its KM staff is considering a balance sheet that would complement the financial balance sheet so that knowledge would be on par with money as a World Bank asset.

Surveys of internal and external end users determine World Bank community effectiveness. Feedback is incongruous because expectations are very different among end-user groups. Internal users are quite particular and difficult to satisfy, and external users often seem relatively easy to please.

But internal survey responses revealed significant improvement within the organization as a result of knowledge management and communities. A majority of staff members have access to the knowledge and information they need, feel encouraged to find new and better ways of working, are satisfied with their ability to communicate with other World Bank staff members, and feel encouraged to disseminate knowledge.

Xerox CEC

The Corporate Engineering Center has measured the impact of the engineering communities on Xerox as a whole. Measures focus on best practices, from product concept to delivery, and on work practices, skills, and tools within engineering and design.

Assessment results reveal that Xerox has tripled its engineering output over the past five years without increasing resources, has dramatically reduced cycle time for new development, and can rapidly iterate derivative products off of existing platforms.

The Xerox software process improvement community also found encouraging results through assessment. Both the number of communities and membership has increased. Because of the community, the amount of time a new software organization takes to progress through developmental levels has decreased significantly, and one software organization reduced its cycle time to 14 months (the industry average is 25.5 months).

Xerox also tracks the number of problems solved. In 2000 Xerox technicians solved 300,000 customer problems using community-driven knowledge. This led to a 5 percent reduction in service hours and a 5 percent reduction in parts costs, estimated at $11.2 million in savings.

Measurement Guidelines

- Make certain that measures accurately reflect your value proposition.
- Measures must be "designed in" to the community of practice.
- Don't create unrealistic expectations about ROI measures.
- Remember that anecdotal measures and stories are useful.
- Be careful what you measure; you just might get it!
- No single measurement system is a magic bullet.
- Meaningful measures are reflective of the goals and objectives of the community.

**KEY LESSONS: COMMUNITY ASSESSMENT
AND MEASUREMENT**

- Measure the health of the community early in its life cycle, but allow some time to grow before trying to measure its effectiveness.
- Use anecdotes and other forms of storytelling to establish the effectiveness of a community.
- Establish an accountability structure that is coordinated with the support structure for the organization.
- Continue to measure the health of the community throughout its life cycle, using trending analysis to spot potential problems.

An Approach to Develop Communities of Practices

Communities of practice, which help knowledge cross the boundaries naturally created by work flow and functions, are emerging as the next step in the evolution of the modern organization. And when a community evolves, it may serve functions other than managing knowledge. It may provide a new, more fluid organization structure that is able to respond with agility to change.

Based on its best-practice research into knowledge management and communities of practice, APQC has developed a road map for developing and implementing successful KM initiatives and communities of practice. Readers familiar with APQC's Stages of Implementation™ will have already discerned that best-practice organizations are following the same five stages as they create and implement their community of practice strategy:

1. Get started
2. Develop Strategy
3. Design and Launch KM Initiatives
4. Expand and Support
5. Institutionalize KM

Stage 1: Get Started

Most organizations began their KM and community initiatives because of a strategic shift in their business model or the basis of competition. For DaimlerChrysler, it was platform teams. For Ford, it was the shift to global standardization of processes. For the World Bank, it was a shift in mission (from a lending bank to a knowledge bank). For Cap Gemini Ernst & Young, it was a decision to compete on knowledge. For Xerox CEC, it was a compelling need to reduce time to market. For Schlumberger, knowledge management is one of three pillars of market strategy.

Stage 2: Develop Strategy

A critical success factor at the second stage is to ensure that a cross-functional leadership group has a hand in setting strategy and selecting the initial communities. Best-practice organizations APQC has examined developed their KM strategy to support the business strategy. The leadership—of the business and the knowledge function—developed a clear picture of how the community approach to KM would support the business model and would help close a knowledge gap that couldn't be easily addressed in the existing structure.

Stage 3: Design and Launch KM Initiatives

At Stage 3, the central KM support team (called different things in different organizations) begins to form and train communities. This support group often forms their own community, such as Siemens' central knowledge management community, and develops their own community tools for sharing lessons and methods.

Experience with these early communities and pilots elevates the visibility and the role of community coordinator or leader and other roles necessary to support and sustain communities.

Stage 4: Expand and Support

Success with their pilots and early communities led best-practice organizations to develop expansion strategies. The critical issues in expansion are the support structure, roles, processes, and resources required.

Stage 5: Institutionalize KM

Communities grow, change, or die; organizations institutionalize. Just because communities fit an organization's business model doesn't mean they will automatically become part of the fabric of organization life. Communities become institutionalized when:

- they fulfill their original intent, both in the minds of members and management;
- the organization provides resources and structure to support the community system; and
- knowledge-sharing behavior becomes an expectation of employees.

FUTURE ISSUES

Working closely with early-adopter organizations in the KM arena since 1995, APQC has been bringing into focus best-practice developments. Communities clearly are bringing new clarity to KM implementation, which substantiates APQC's earlier predictions that communities were the route to rich knowledge.

As communities become more tightly woven into the fabric of organizations and their "voice" in an organization grows, potential issues emerge. The dilemma for communities is how to take on an expanded, institutional role in the organization without losing their organic character.

Keeping Communities from Becoming Bureaucratic and Rigid

- Keep the voluntary character of communities. When they become bureaucratic, they will lose members, influence, and life. Less bureaucratic communities will rise to take their place.

- Communities that preserve their informal character have an edge.
- As communities become a more integral part of the organization, they begin to reshape the organization itself by changing the culture to one of greater knowledge sharing. This could provide some resistance to bureaucratization altogether.

Keeping Communities from Breaking with the Organizational Structure and Becoming an Isolated Subculture

Most knowledge-stewarding communities desire a voice in the organization. Although the occasional community becomes renegade, most will support an organization's mission. Members will likely report to the primary structure and find their career path there as well. Most communities want to become integrated into day-to-day work. The more integrated they are, the less likely they are to split off and lose contact with the main organization. The KM steering team also provides the link that prevents this isolation.

Keeping the Rest of the Organization from Resenting the Level of Voice Communities Request

This issue has not emerged yet, but could. As more knowledge workers and managers participate in communities, fewer people are left out who could resent the community.

Cross-organization Communities

Organizations are increasingly seeking ways to manage and support activities that transcend traditional boundaries. We've talked about that challenge here in terms of enabling communities of practice that cut across particular functional, organizational, or geographical boundaries within an enterprise.

The next challenge is to extend this concept beyond the organization to encompass prospects and customers, partners and suppliers, and other key stakeholders and value creators. Organizational boundaries—the distinctions that separate organizations, their partners, and their customers—are beginning to blur. The boundaries that have traditionally separated organizations from these entities are becoming increasingly porous.

By collaborating with their customers and prospects through interactive marketing and mass customization, companies will more effectively pinpoint customer needs and preferences. Interaction of this sort enables an organization to create more innovative and personalized offerings and build more loyal and profitable customer relationships.

Of course, new technology is both enabling new forms of collaboration and, by raising expectations, making such activities commonplace. Communication technology, transportation, and logistics make it easy to collaborate and coordinate. Instead of vertical integration, companies such as Dell now tout "virtual integration," a business strategy focused on building dynamic relationships with suppliers and partners (instead of just buying and subsuming them).

As traditional communities embrace new member bases, electronic communities emerge online. Alongside hobbyists and affinity groups in chat rooms are trading communities such as eBay and Yahoo!. EBay, for instance, encourages communication among members through discussion boards. Although discussion boards are not considered part of the community, the company builds trust and loyalty by providing a platform for relationship building. On a large scale, we find the emergence of collaborative exchanges that unite buyers and sellers online. Categorizing such activities at this point is difficult, but the Internet will inevitably propel collaborative activities that cross traditional organizational boundaries. It has the potential to make the concepts of external and internal knowledge seem less important and less clear.

Consider Dell Computer. It strengthens its connections to customers and suppliers by sharing information and deepening relationships. It depends on customers—particularly large enterprise clients—to share their complex technology needs and expectations. It depends on suppliers—whether for monitors, motherboards, or flat panel displays—to become an integral part of its own production processes. In a sense, the company has built communities extending into the supply chain. Such relationships reduce inventory, cut costs, and enable Dell to respond to customer needs with customized solutions.

Many models for communities of practice extend beyond any one particular organization. Professional and trade associations have long provided forums and support for like-minded individuals to exchange ideas and learn from each other. Academic communities have offered another model that revolves around publishing and peer review. And technology companies have built customer communities through user groups and conferences.

One might expect such models to be enhanced by the Internet. It enlarges our sphere of potential interactions, and as Web tools become more collaborative, they become more useful in a community-building sense. We are increasingly able to share insights, ideas, multimedia files, charts, graphics; and we are able to see and speak to each other through real-time audio and video.

Although the value of convening and meeting face-to-face will remain critical, we can expect such interpersonal activities to be highly complemented by communication technology and virtual community building, thus enabling the globalization of communities.

We must prepare to embrace these types of trends. Organizations can strengthen relationships by building communities that encompass the various participants in the value-creation process. The communities will continue to overcome barriers in order to accelerate knowledge transfer and expand opportunities for trade and success.

About the Authors

Farida Hasanali

A project manager with significant experience in knowledge management, Farida Hasanali has served in several roles at APQC over the past eight years. She has led and been involved in numerous consortium studies, including four that focused on knowledge management.

Hasanali, whose expertise includes information technology and knowledge management, led the design and development of APQC's Knowledge Sharing Network, which is a collaborative environment for APQC member organizations to network and access research.

A presenter at several knowledge management events, Hasanali holds a bachelor's degree in psychology from St. Xavier College in Bombay, India.

Cindy Hubert

Director of knowledge management and learning at the American Productivity & Quality Center, Cindy Hubert has played an instrumental role in building APQC's reputation as a leader in the KM arena. She and her team have worked with more than 250 organizations to provide KM assessments, strategy development, project management, and internal and external benchmarking studies.

A frequent speaker on knowledge management issues and best practices at conferences in the United States and abroad, Hubert has played an instrumental role in the development and delivery of APQC's knowledge management education and curriculum. Her role encompasses all of APQC's Connected Learning™ offerings covering such topics as KM, benchmarking, performance measurement, and process improvement. In addition to developing a practitioner certification program, Hubert directs APQC's on-site, custom, and computer-based training offerings.

Prior to being named director of knowledge management and learning, Hubert served as a senior consultant in knowledge management and manager of APQC's KM practice area, focusing on business process improvement including knowledge management, transfer of best practices, quality, benchmarking, measurement, and strategic planning.

An instructor in Knowledge Management & the Transfer of Best Practices at Rice University's Executive Education Graduate School of Management, Hubert is a graduate of the University of Texas at Austin. She earned a bachelor's degree in business administration and marketing with emphasis in accounting and finance.

Kimberly Lopez

Kimberly Lopez is a senior knowledge management specialist with the American Productivity & Quality Center. Since joining APQC in 1998, she has been involved in numerous individual and consortium studies in the areas of higher education, human resources, and knowledge management. She has worked with several organizations to develop knowledge management strategies and approaches for organizational improvement.

Prior to working at APQC, Lopez served in the intellectual property area. Her positions included intellectual property system consultant for a leading online information company and program coordinator for the University of Houston Law Center's intellectual property program. She has been a guest lecturer on various property-related topics.

Lopez holds a bachelor's degree in political science from the University of St. Thomas and an MBA from the University of Houston.

Bob Newhouse

Bob Newhouse is a senior advisor specializing in knowledge management and performance improvement at the American Productivity & Quality Center. With a focus on knowledge management, transfer of best practices, process improvement, and quality systems implementation across a variety of public- and private-sector organizations, Newhouse works with organizations to design and implement knowledge documentation and transfer processes based on research conducted by APQC.

After joining APQC in 1995, Newhouse led an APQC team responsible for the design and implementation of best practice transfer and benchmarking tools for education. He also helped schools and universities understand and use the Baldrige Quality Award Criteria as a tool for improvement. He has managed a variety of projects and training programs with executives and managers of Fortune 500 companies. Additionally, Newhouse has led both process and metric benchmarking studies in the areas of measurement, corporate universities, customer satisfaction measurement, customer service, order management, customer call centers, and facilities operations. Newhouse, who has served as a Texas Quality Award examiner since 1998, also has published several articles and made numerous conference presentations.

Newhouse holds a bachelor's degree from the University of Notre Dame. He received a Doctor of Jurisprudence from the University of Houston Law Center and is licensed to practice law in the state of Texas.

Carla O'Dell, Ph.D.

Dr. Carla O'Dell is president of the American Productivity & Quality Center and serves as director of its International Benchmarking Clearinghouse.

Dr. O'Dell's work in knowledge management dates back to 1995, when APQC launched, under her direction, its first knowledge management consortium study, Emerging Best Practices in Knowledge Management, with 39 organizations. She also led APQC's second study, Using Information Technology to Support Knowledge Management, with 25 of the world's leading KM organizations and has been active in APQC's eight subsequent consortium studies as well as individual company projects.

Dr. O'Dell is co-author with Dr. C. Jackson Grayson of *American Business: A Two-Minute Warning*, which Tom Peters said "gets my vote as the best business book in 1988." Also with Dr. Grayson, Dr. O'Dell co-authored *If Only We Knew What We Know: The Transfer of Internal Knowledge and Best Practice*, published in 1998 by Simon & Schuster. She publishes several business journal articles each year.

A frequent keynote speaker at senior executive events who appears often on business television, Dr. O'Dell holds a bachelor's degree from Stanford University, a master's degree from the University of Oregon, and a Ph.D. in industrial and organization psychology from the University of Houston.

Wesley Vestal

Wesley Vestal, a knowledge management specialist at the American Productivity & Quality Center, has worked extensively in designing and implementing knowledge management strategies, solutions, and systems for organizations such as Best Buy, Schlumberger and the American Cancer Society. Vestal speaks at knowledge management conferences across the United States, South America, and Europe and is also an APQC-certified trainer in knowledge management and benchmarking skills. Additionally, he has managed process and metric benchmarking studies in the areas of knowledge management, technology-based training, leadership development, performance management, information technology systems, shared services, accountability systems in K–12 schools, and faculty instructional development.

Prior to joining APQC, Vestal spent four years at the United Way of the Texas Gulf Coast, where he served in a business development capacity and advised the largest donor companies on developing and growing their charitable giving efforts. In addition to raising more than $15 million as manager of new business development and major campaigns, he served as a corporate trainer, facilitator, and advisor.

Vestal holds a bachelor's degree in history and political science from Trinity University in San Antonio.

About APQC

F ounded in 1977, the Houston-based American Productivity &
Quality Center provides the knowledge, training, and methods
that empower businesses and other organizations to maximize their
potential with a focus on productivity, quality, and best practices.
APQC is a nonprofit organization and an internationally recognized
leader in benchmarking and best-practice information, serving its
500-plus members and other customers in all sectors of business,
industry, education, and government.

Over the years APQC has built a distinguished list of achieve-
ments, including providing private-sector input into the first White
House Conference on Productivity and spearheading the 1987
creation of the Malcolm Baldrige National Quality Award, which
we jointly administered for its first three years. In 1992 we created
the International Benchmarking Clearinghouse, a comprehensive
service co-designed with customers to facilitate benchmarking.
Our most recent venture is the APQC Education Initiative, a
special program designed to integrate business best practices into
educational institutions.

Today, APQC continues to work with organizations to improve
productivity and quality by providing the tools, information, and
support they need to discover and implement best practices and
obtain results in dozens of process areas.

For information on the many ways APQC can help meet your
organization's knowledge management and process improvement
needs, call 800-776-9676 (713-681-4020 outside the United States)
or visit our Web site at www.apqc.org. To see additional publications,
go to www.store.apqc.org.